REALLY

DIRTY
JOKES

Other titles in this series:

REALLY WICKED

DIRTY JOKES

Compiled by David Brown

MICHAEL O'MARA BOOKS LTD

First published in Great Britain in 1998
by Michael O'Mara Books Limited
9 Lion Yard
Tremadoc Road
London SW4 7NQ

A CIP catalogue record for this book is available from the British Library

ISBN 1-85479-373-X

1 3 5 7 9 10 8 6 4 2

Cover design by Powerfresh

Designed and typeset by Design 23

Printed and bound in Great Britain by Cox & Wyman, Reading, Berks.

DEFINE YOUR TERMS!

Three men were on a trip to Saudi Arabia. One day, they came upon a harem with over 100 beautiful women. They started getting friendly with all the women, when suddenly the Sheikh came in.

"I am the master of all these women," he said, "No-one else can touch them except me. You three men must all pay for what you have done today. You will each die, but in the way that corresponds with your profession."

The Sheikh turned to the first man and asked him what he did for a living.

"I'm a police marksman," said the first man.

"Alright, shoot his penis off!" ordered the Sheikh.

He then turned to the second man and asked him what he did for a living.

"I'm a fireman," said the second man.

"Alright, burn his penis off!" ordered the Sheik.

Finally, he asked the last man, "And you, what do you do for a living?"

And the third man answered, with a big smile on his face,

"I'm a lollipop salesman!"

A man and a woman started to have sex in the middle of a dark forest. After 15 minutes of this, the man finally got up and said, "Damn, I wish I had a torch." The woman says, "So do I. You've been eating grass for the past ten minutes!"

In the middle of his university course, a young man came to terms with his homosexuality and decided to come out of the closet. His plan was to tell his mother first; so, on his next home visit, he went to the kitchen, where his mother was busying herself stirring the stew with a wooden spoon.

Rather nervously, he explained to her that while he was at university, he had realized he was gay.

Without looking up from her stew, his mother said,

'You mean, you're homosexual?'

'Well...yes.'

Still without looking up: 'Does that mean you have other men's cocks in your mouth?'

Caught off guard, the young man eventually managed to stammer an embarrassed affirmative.

His mother turned to him and, brandishing the wooden spoon threateningly under his nose, snapped:

'Right! Don't you EVER complain about my cooking again!'

The stages of a woman's life:

Below the age of 14, she is like Antarctica: untouchable.

Between the ages of 14 and 17, she is like Africa: virgin and unexplored.

Between the ages of 18 and 30, she is like Asia: hot and exotic.

Between the ages of 30 and 45, she is like America: fully explored, breathtakingly beautiful and free with her resources.

Between the ages of 46 and 56, she is like Europe: exhausted but still with points of interest.

After 56, she is like Australia: everybody knows it's down there, but nobody gives a damn.

There was this bar in need of a piano player, so the manager hung a 'Piano Player Wanted' sign in the window. An hour or so later, a man walks in and asks to audition. The manager tells him to go ahead and play something. The man sits down and begins to play the greatest music the manager has ever heard.

Tears are welling up in his eyes as the man ends the song. The manager tells the man that it was the best thing he's ever heard and asks for the name of the song.

The man says, "I wrote that song. I call it 'Two guys having sex'." The manager winces, but before he can say anything, the man starts to play an even more beautiful song.

This time, when he ends, the manager is weeping.

Wiping away a tear, he tells the man that it was the loveliest song he's ever heard.

The man says, "I wrote that song too. I call it 'Six guys having sex with one really fat chick'."

The manager winces again but arrives at a solution.

He tells the man the job is his, but he must never tell the customers the names of the songs. The man understands and agrees to start the next night at 9:00 pm.

The next night, 9:00 pm rolls around and the man hasn't shown up. At 9:05 he comes charging through the door with his dress shirt unbuttoned, his flies open and his cock hanging out of his trousers. He races over to the piano and proceeds to play the most beautiful music anyone has ever heard. The manager calls one of his waitresses over and tells her to tell the man that his flies are undone and his cock is showing. The waitress makes her way over to the man and whispers in his ear, "Do you know your flies are open and your cock is sticking out?"

The man replies, "Know it, I wrote it!"

The other day we all went to this club. One of the guys wanted to impress us, so he pulled out a £10 note. The nude dancer came over to us, and my friend licked the £10 note and put it on her backside. Not to be outdone, my other friend pulled out a £50 note. He called the girl back over, licked the £50 note and stuck it on her other cheek.

Now all the attention was focused on me. What could I do to top that? I got out my wallet, thought for a minute – then the financial genius in my soul took over.

I got out my cash card, swiped it down her crack, grabbed the £60 and went home.

A woman walks into her accountant's office and tells him that she needs to complete her tax return.

The accountant says, "Before we begin, I'll need to ask a few questions." He gets her name, address and national insurance number, etc. and then asks, "What is your occupation?"

The woman replies, "I'm a whore."
The accountant baulks and says, "No, no, no. That will never do. That is much too crass. Let's try to rephrase that."
The woman says, "Okay then, I'm a prostitute."
"No, that is still too crude. Try again."
They both think for a minute, then the woman states, "I'm a chicken farmer."
The accountant asks, "What does chicken farming have to do with being a whore or a prostitute?"
"Well, I raised over 5,000 cocks last year."

The Seven Most Important Men in a Woman's Life

1. The Doctor – who tells her to "take off all your clothes".

2. The Dentist – who tells her to "open wide".

3. The Milkman – who asks her "do you want it delivered to the front or the back?"

4. The Hairdresser – who asks her "do you want it teased or blown?".

5. The Interior Designer – who assures her "once it's inside, you'll love it!".

6. The Banker – who insists to her "if you take it out too soon, you'll lose interest!".

7. The Primal Hunter – who always goes deep into the bush, always shoots twice, always eats what he shoots, but keeps telling her "keep quiet, and lie still!".

There was a young lady from Ealing
Who professed to lack sexual feeling
Till a lady named Doris
Just touched her clitoris
And she had to be scraped off the ceiling.

ANIMAL PASSIONS

Two ducks booked into a hotel for a night of passion but, as they were starting to get undressed, they realized that they had forgotten their condoms. So the male duck called room service and asked if they could send one up. Within a few minutes a waiter arrived bearing a condom on a silver tray.

The waiter said to the male duck, "Shall I put it on your bill, sir?"

And the male duck said angrily, "Certainly not. What do you think I am – some kind of pervert?"

A man takes his parrot to the vet. He says, "You may find it hard to believe, but I think my parrot is feeling sexy."

"Feeling sexy?" asks the vet. "How can you tell?"

"I wanna get laid. I wanna get laid," the parrot starts squawking.

The vet says, "I guess he must be feeling sexy. I have a female parrot here. For £30, I'll put her in the cage with your bird."

The parrot says, "Pay him. Pay him."

So the owner gives the vet £30.

The vet takes the female parrot and puts it inside the cage with the delighted male parrot, then covers the cage.

Moments later, there is a lot of squawking and screaming and feathers are flying everywhere. The vet lifts the cover off the cage. Inside the male parrot is holding the female parrot down with one claw and ripping her feathers out with the other.

The parrot is screeching, "For £30, I expect you to take your clothes off!"

My father's stories about the birds and the bees were so fascinating, I was 29 before I got interested in girls.

What did the elephant say to the man with a ten-inch cock?

"Very nice, but can you eat peanuts with it?"

There were three dogs, all in the dog pound. The first dog turned to the second dog and asked,

"What are you in for?" The dog replied, "Well my master said that if I kept on chewing up the newspapers he would have me put me to sleep. I kept chewing them and so today I'm being put to sleep."

The other dogs started to comfort him.

The second dog turned to the third dog and asked him the same question. The dog sadly replied, "Well my master said that if I kept drinking out of the toilet I would get put to sleep. And I didn't stop, so here I am about to be put to sleep."

The other dogs started to comfort him too. Then the second and third dog turned to the first dog and asked him what had happened. The dog said, "When my owner got out of the shower, her towel fell off, and when she bent over, I just couldn't help myself and started to have sex with her."

The dogs understood immediately, and said,

"Oh, well, we're not surprised that you're getting put to sleep."

The first dog turned around and said, "Who said I'm here to get put to sleep? I'm here to get my claws trimmed!"

What did the nymphomaniac say when her dog started licking her face?

"Down boy!"

A lonely woman was in the pet shop looking for an unusual pet to keep her company. The pet shop owner brought her a frog and said,

"This frog has been specially trained to perform thrilling sex with a woman. You can have him for a low, low price – just £500!"

The woman bought the frog, took it home, and lay down on the floor with her legs open. The frog did nothing.

The woman angrily returned to the pet shop and complained about the frog's non-performance.

"Show me what you did," said the pet shop owner.

So the woman lay on the floor with her legs open. The frog just sat there doing nothing.

The pet shop owner came over to the woman, put his face between her legs, and yelled to the frog, "All right, you little moron, this is the last time I am going to show you!"

An English anthropologist was walking down the road of an American Indian reservation camp. Along the way he met an Indian with a feather on his head. He asked the Indian, "Excuse me! What does that feather mean?"

The Indian answered, "This feather means I had sex with one squaw."

"Oooh," remarked the Englishman. He went on his way again until he met another Indian with five feathers on his head.

He queried, "Excuse me! What do those five feathers mean?"

"These five feathers mean that I have had sex with five squaws." said the Indian proudly.

"Oh, I see," said the Englishman, and he continued on his way again until he met another Indian with ten feathers on his head and he asked him the same question.

The Indian replied, "These feathers mean I have had sex with TEN squaws!"

"Ooohh, interesting," nodded the Englishman.

And the Indian added, "You should see village chief."

So off the Englishman went to see the chief.

He approached the chief who was wearing

his crown of feathers and asked, "Hey, Chief! What do all those feathers mean?"

With a flourish, the chief said proudly, "These feathers mean I have had sex with the WHOLE VILLAGE!"

"Whole Village! Holy cow!" gasped the Englishman.

"Yes, cows too," added the chief.

"But aren't they hostile?" asked the Englishman.

"Horse-style, doggy-style, any style," said the chief dismissively.

"Oh, dear," said the Englishman.

"No. No deer. Not possible. Ass too high," replied the chief.

When man was first made, he was given only 20 years of normal sex life. Naturally, he was horrified! Only 20 years!

The monkey also was given 20 years, but said that ten years was plenty. The man asked for the monkey's other ten years and they were given to him.

The lion was also given 20 years, but he also said he only needed ten years. Again, man asked for the other ten years, and the lion agreed.

Then came the donkey, and he was also given 20 years but, like the other animals, ten years was enough for him.

And again man asked for, and was given, ten more years.

Now, this explains why man today has 20 years of normal sex life, then ten years of monkeying around, ten years of lion about it and last of all ten years of making an ass of himself.

There were two baby whales in the ocean – one baby boy whale and one baby girl whale. They played together every day in the ocean. One day the boy whale saw an oil freighter in the water. "Look, that is the boat that killed my father," said the boy whale. "We have to do something! I have to avenge my father's death! Are you with me?" The girl whale just stared at the boy.

"Look," he said, "I bet if we swim under the boat and blow from our blow holes hard enough, we can tip that awful boat over and avenge my father's death. Now, are you with me?"

The girl whale wanted to help the boy whale, so she said, "Okay."

So the two baby whales swam under the freighter and they blew from their blow holes as hard as they could. Sure enough, the boat tipped over.

"At last! I have avenged my father's death," said the boy whale.

But then they noticed there were some sailors swimming around in the water.

"Look", said the boy whale, "There are survivors. We can't let that happen. I have to avenge my father's death."

"What do you want to do now?" asked the girl.

"Well, we have to swim over there and eat them of course," said the boy whale.

"Whoa... wait a minute," said the girl whale, "I was with you for the blow job, but I'm not swallowing any seamen."

YOU'RE

KIDDING!

There was a fourth-form boy and a fourth-form girl.

The boy went over to the girl's house with a football and teased her saying,

"Ha Ha! You can't have a football 'cos you're just a girl."

The girl went to her mum crying, so her mum bought her a football. The boy got angry.

So the next day he came over with a boy's bike and teased her saying,

"Ha Ha! You can't have a boy's bike 'cos you're just a girl!"

So the girl went crying to her mum and she got a boy's bike.

The boy became very cross. So the next day he went over, pulled down his pants and said,

"I have one of these and you can't go crying to your mum to get one of your own!"

The girl went crying to her mum and then a little later came out, pulled up her dress and said,

"My mum said as long as I have one of these I can get as many of those as I want!"

One day a little boy went to school and the teacher said, "For homework, I want you to find out the difference between 'hypothetically' and 'realistically'."

So the boy went home and asked his father, "Dad, what's the difference between "hypothetically' and 'realistically'?"

His father replied, "Ask you mother if she'd sleep with somebody for a million pounds."

His son looked at his father in a bewildered fashion, but proceeded to do as he was told.

"Mum, would you sleep with someone for a million pounds?"

The mother replied, "Well, son, that is quite a large sum of money – I think I would."

So the son went back to his father and said, "Dad, Mum said she would do it, but I just don't understand, what does that have to do with 'hypothetically' and 'realistically'?"

The father replied, "Don't worry about it, just ask your sister if she'd do it."

The boy went and asked his sister. She replied,

"A million pounds? OF COURSE I WOULD DO IT!!"

So, the boy returned once again to his father saying,

"Dad, she said she'd do it too, but I still don't understand, what does that have to do with 'hypothetically' and 'realistically'?"

The father replied, "Well son, HYPO-THETICALLY we're sitting on two million pounds, REALISTICALLY, we're living with a couple of whores!"

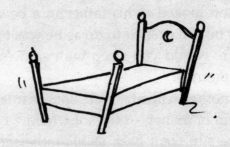

A little boy walks in on his parents having sex. He says, "What are you both doing?"

His mum says, "Well I was just letting the air out of your dad, because he's much too fat."

The boy says,"Why? The lady next door is only going to blow him up again!"

A little girl runs out to the backyard where her father is working, and asks him, "Daddy, what's sex?"

Her father thinks, "OK! It's time for that sort of question, is it? Right then, here we go!" So he takes a deep breath, sits her down, and tells her all about the birds and the bees. He tells her about conception, sexual intercourse, sperm and eggs. He goes on to tell her about puberty, menstruation, erections, wet-dreams...and he thinks, what the hell, and goes on to tell her the complete works.

He covers a wide and varied assortment of sub-topics and by the time he's finished, his daughter is somewhat awestruck with this sudden influx of bizarre new knowledge. Her father finally asks: "But what did you want to know about sex for?"

"Oh, mummy said to tell you lunch would be ready in a couple of secs..."

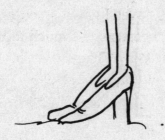

A married couple took their son on holiday and went to a nude beach. The father went for a walk on the beach and the son went to play in the water.

The son came running up to his mummy and said, "Mummy, I saw ladies with boobies a lot bigger than yours!"

His mum said, "The bigger they are, the stupider they are."

So he went back to play. Minutes later he ran back and says, "Mummy, I saw men with cocks a lot bigger than Daddy's!" His mum says, "The bigger they are, the stupider they are."

So he went back to play. Several minutes later he came running back and said,

"Mummy, I just saw Daddy talking to the stupidest lady I ever saw and the more and more he talked to her, the stupider and stupider he got!"

Son: "Dad, I have to do a special essay for school. What's politics?"

Father: "Well, let's take our home for example. I am the wage-earner, so let's call me management. Your mother is the administrator of the money, so we'll call her government. We take care of your needs, so let's call you the people. We'll call the maid the working class and as for your baby brother we'll call him the future. Do you understand?"

Son: "I'm not really sure, Dad. I'll have to think about it."

That night, woken up by his baby brother's crying, the boy went to see what was wrong. Discovering the baby had seriously soiled his nappy, the boy went to his parents' room and found his mother sound asleep. He then went to the maid's room where, peeking through the key hole, he saw his father in bed with the maid. The boy's knocking went totally unheard by his father and the maid, so the boy returned to his room and went back to bed.

The next morning the son said:

"Dad, now I think I understand politics."

Father: "That's great son, explain it to me in your own words!"

Son: "Well, Dad, while management is screwing the working class, the government is sound asleep. The people are being completely ignored and the future is full of sh*t!"

One day little Johnny went to his father and asked him if he could buy him a £100 bicycle for his birthday. Johnny's father said, "We have an £80,000 mortgage on the house, and you want me to buy you a bicycle? Wait until Christmas."

Christmas came around and Johnny asked again.

The father said, "Well, the mortgage is still extremely high. Sorry about that. Ask me again some other time."

About two days later, the boy was seen walking out of the house with all of his worldly possessions in a suitcase. The father asked him why he was leaving. Little Johnny said, "Yesterday I was walking past your room and I heard you say that you were pulling out, and Mummy said that you should wait because she was coming too – and I'll be damned if I'm going to get stuck with an £80,000 mortgage!"

The teacher had a new assignment for the class. She told them to draw a beautiful picture and explain why it was beautiful.

So the next day, little Teddy showed the teacher his picture of a beautiful landscape. He told her that it was beautiful because every summer he and his parents went there to have a picnic and his parents always said that it was the most beautiful place to have a picnic.

The teacher said, "Very good Teddy, you get an A."

So it was little Ricky's turn to show his picture. It was a picture of a lake. He told the teacher that this was a beautiful picture because every summer he and his father went fishing there and every time his father would tell him that this was the most beautiful place to fish.

The teacher said again, "Very good Ricky, you also get an A."

So it was Johnny's turn to show *his* beautiful picture. It had a dot in the middle of the page. The teacher asked, "What on earth is so beautiful about this?"

He told her that last night his sister told her dad that she hadn't had her period in a month, and his dad had said,

"That's beautiful, that's just f**king beautiful!"

A teacher is helping her students with a maths problem. She tells them the following story: "There are three birds sitting on a wire. A gunman shoots one of the birds. How many birds are left on the wire?" A boy pauses. "None," he replied thoughtfully.

"No, no, no, Let's try again," the teacher says patiently. She holds up three fingers. "There are three birds sitting on a wire. A gunman shoots one," she puts down one finger, "how many birds are left on the wire?"

"None," the boy says with authority.

The teacher sighs. "Tell me how you came up with that."

"It's simple," says the boy, "after the gunman shot one bird, he scared the wits out of the other two and they flew away."

"Well," she says, "it's not technically correct, but I must say I like the way you think."

"Okay," chimes the boy, "now let me ask you a question. There are three women sitting on a bench eating ice lollies. One woman is licking the ice lolly, one woman is biting the ice lolly, and one is sucking the ice lolly. Which one is married?" he ask innocently.

The teacher looks at the boy's angelic face and

writhes in agony, turning three shades of red.

"C'mon," the boy says impatiently, "one is licking the lolly, one is biting and one is sucking. Which one is married?"

"Well," she gulps and, in a barely audible whisper, replies, "The one who's sucking?"

"No," he says with surprise, "It's the one wearing the wedding ring. But I like the way you think."

A little girl came running into the house crying her eyes out and cradling her hand: "Mummy, quick! Get me a glass of cider!" she wailed.

"Why do you want a glass of cider, darling?" asked her mum.

"I cut my hand on a thorn, and I want the pain to go away!"

Confused, but hoping to stop the child's crying, the mother obliged and poured her a glass of cider. The little girl immediately put her hand in it.

"Ouch! It still hurts! This cider doesn't work!" complained the little girl.

"What are you talking about?" asked her puzzled mother.

"Well, I overheard big sister say that whenever she gets a prick in her hand, she just has to get it in cider."

Bill and Mary Jones decided that the only way to manage a Sunday afternoon quickie while their ten-year-old son was in the flat was to send him outside on to the balcony and get him to report on all the neighbourhood activities.

The boy began his commentary as his parents put their plan into operation. "There's a car being towed from the car park," he said.

"An ambulance just drove by." A few moments passed. "Looks like the Andersons have visitors," he called out. "Jim's riding a new bike and the Coopers are having sex."

His mum and dad shot up in bed. "How do you know that?" the startled father asked.

"Their Jimmy Cooper is standing out on the balcony too," his son replied.

NATURAL

MISTAKES

Two sperm are swimming along and one is beginning to get tired. He asks his friend, "How far do you think it is to the uterus? I'm getting pretty tired."

His friend says, "I'm not sure, but I think it must be a long way yet – we've only just passed the oesophagus."

Two women on a business trip were sharing a hotel room. The first night, after the lights were out, one of them came over to the other's bed and started to caress her shoulder.

"There's something I want to tell you, and I don't know how to say it, so I'll just be frank ..." Rising from her bed, the other woman interrupted, "No, I'll be Frank."

An old man, staring mournfully at his cock, intoned: "We were born together. We grew up together. We got married together. Why, oh why, did you have to die before me?"

A notice in the bedroom of an Italian hotel:

'Do not adjust your light hanger. If you wish to have it off the manageress will oblige you.'

A man was walking along the road when he saw a ladder going into the clouds. As any of us would, he started to climb the ladder. He reached a fluffy white cloud, upon which sat a rather plump and very ugly woman.

"Have sex with me or climb the ladder to success," she said.

No contest, thought the man and he climbed the ladder to the next cloud. On this cloud was a slightly thinner woman, who was rather easier on the eye.

"Make love to me or climb the ladder to success," she said. "Well," thought the man, "I might as well carry on."

On the next cloud was an even nicer woman who, this time, was quite attractive.

"Have sex with me now or climb the ladder to success," she said in gentle tones..

But he turned her down and went on up the ladder.

He thought to himself that the women were actually getting better the further up the ladder he went.

On the next cloud was an absolute beauty. Slim, attractive, the lot!

"Take me here and now or climb the ladder to success," she said.

Imagining what gorgeous creature would be waiting next, and being a gambling man, he decided to climb again.

When he reached the next cloud, there was an enormously fat ugly man, covered in hair, with flies buzzing around his head.

"Who are you?" the man asked.

"Hello" said the ugly fat man, "I'm Cess!"

A truck driver came upon a couple making passionate love in the middle of the road. He almost jumped out of his skin with fright.

He blew his horn, blinked his lights and yet the couple didn't miss a stroke!

The driver stopped, got out and shouted at them, "Are you crazy, didn't you hear my horn, see my lights, didn't you know I was coming?"

The excited young man said, "Yes, I knew you were coming! I knew she was coming and I knew I was coming! I also knew you were the only one here with brakes!"

Two old ladies were sitting on a bench together in Miami, both smoking cigarettes. One of the old ladies took out a condom and put it on her cigarette.

The other old lady looked at her and asked her why on earth she was doing that. The other old lady replied that it was supposed to be a safer way to smoke.

The next day the first old lady went to a pharmacy and asked the assistant for a condom. The assistant asked her what colour and she replied that it didn't matter.

Then the assistant asked her what size condom she needed and she said,

"I want one that will fit a Camel."

Pierre, the brave French fighter pilot, takes his girlfriend, Marie, out for a pleasant little picnic by the River Seine.

It's a beautiful day and love is in the air. Marie leans over to Pierre and says: "Pierre, my cheri, kiss me!"

Our hero grabs a bottle of Merlot and splashes it on Marie's lips. "What are you doing, Pierre?", says the startled Marie.

"I am Pierre the fighter pilot! When I have red meat, I like to have red wine!"

She smiles and they start kissing. When things began to get a little passionate, Marie says, "Pierre, kiss me lower down."

Our hero tears her blouse open, grabs a bottle of Chardonnay and starts pouring it all over her breasts.

"Pierre! What are you doing?" asks the bewildered Marie.

"I am Pierre the fighter pilot! When I have white meat, I like to have white wine!"

They resume their passionate interlude and things really get steamy!. Marie leans close to his ear and whispers, "Pierre, kiss me lower down!"

Our hero rips off her underwear, grabs a bottle of Cognac and pours it in her lap. He then strikes a match and sets the Cognac alight.

Marie shrieks and dives into the river. Standing waist deep, Marie throws her arms upwards and screams furiously,

"PIERRE, WHAT IN THE HELL DO YOU THINK YOU'RE DOING?"

Our hero stands up, defiantly, and says, "I am Pierre the fighter pilot! When I go down, I go down in flames!"

A young man talked his 90-year old father into going to a nursing home.

"It's clean, friendly, you'll meet people your own age, they'll take care of you and I won't have to worry about you being alone." said the son.

So the old man decided to try it out for a week. The very first morning he woke up with an erection. A beautiful nurse came into his room and noticed this. So she took her clothes off and made love to him. When the nurse had finished she put her clothes back on and left with a cheerful wave.

The old man called his son on the phone:

"Son! This place is wonderful! I'm so glad you talked me into this. I'm never going to leave, I want to die here!"

After he spoken to his son the old man put on his dressing gown and slippers and walked down the corridor wearing a big smile. He was so excited that he wasn't paying attention.

Suddenly he slipped and fell flat on his face.

A male orderly saw this and rushed over to him. Then he lifted up the back of the old man's dressing gown and proceeded to have passionate sex with him.

The old man was too frail to resist. When the orderly had finished the old man crawled back to his room, reached for the phone and called his son:

"Help me, son! This place is killing me! You've got to get me out of here right away. I'm going to die here!"

The son says: "Hold on dad, only 20 minutes ago you were saying how much you liked it! Now all of a sudden you've changed your mind. What's been happening?"

After explaining the sequence of events that morning the old man says: "You see son, my problem is, I only get an erection once a year but I fall down three times a day."

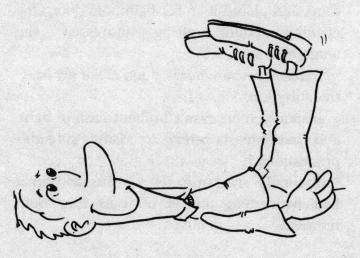

A Philadelphia truck driver is driving down the road, when he sees a large sign that says CLOCKS.

He pulls over to the side of the road, runs into the store, whips his cock out and slams it on the counter.

Calmly, the store attendant explains,

"Sorry, sir, the sign outside says CLOCKS, not COCKS."

The truck driver says, "Yes. I know – just put two hands and a face on it, and I'll be happy!"

A young woman bought a mirror at an antique shop, and placed it on her bathroom door. One evening, while getting undressed, she laughingly said,

"Mirror, mirror, on my door, make my bust-size forty-four."

Instantly, there was a brilliant flash of light, and her breasts grew to really splendid proportions.

Excitedly, she ran to tell her husband what had happened, and in minutes they both returned.

The husband crossed his fingers and said, "Mirror, mirror on the door, make my cock touch the floor!"

Again, there was a bright flash ...... and both his legs fell off.

Three men were sleeping in the same bed. In the morning they started discussing their dreams.

The man on the right said, "I had a dream that I was getting a hand job."

The man on the left said, "I had a dream that I was getting a hand job too."

Then the man in the middle said,

"That's really weird, I had a dream that I was skiing."

A 92-year-old woman and a 94-year-old man lived in a nursing home. They had been 'special' friends for five years.

Every night they would get into bed together. She would take his cock in her hand and just hold it.

They would fall asleep happily this way.

One day as the old lady was walking through the home she came across her gentleman friend in bed with another woman.

She was thoroughly distraught and screamed at him, "I've been sleeping with you for five years and now you betray me! What does she have that I don't?"

The old man replied, "Parkinsons."

A man was travelling through the Arizona desert when he came upon an Indian lying on the ground stark naked, with an erection sticking straight up in the air.

He asked the Indian what he was doing, and the Indian replied, "I'm telling the time."

The man told the Indian that he didn't believe him, so the Indian told him that it was 1:00 p.m.

The man looked at his watch and was completely amazed to find that it was, indeed, exactly 1:00 p.m.

He travelled a bit further on until he came upon yet another naked Indian lying on the ground, with an erection sticking straight up.

He asked this Indian what he was doing and he, too, replied that he was telling the time. He asked the Indian to prove it, and the Indian told him that it was exactly 2:00 p.m.

The man looked at his watch and once again is astonished to find that the time was correct.

He continued his trek through the desert until he came across an Indian lying naked in the sand, rubbing his cock. He said to this Indian, "And what the hell are you doing?"

To which the Indian replied, "I'm winding my watch."

There was this man who had a girlfriend he loved so much, he had her name tattooed on his cock.

When unaroused all you could see were the letters WY.

One day he was in a public toilet when a big black guy came up to use the urinal next to him.

Being a bit curious he looked down and, to his amazement, saw the letters WY tattooed on the other guy's cock.

"Hey, I have a tattoo just like that, is your girlfriend's name Wendy as well?"

"Nah, mine says 'Welcome to Jamaica, have a nice day', that's all." replied his neighbour with a big smile.

One day a man decided to go for a ride in his van. He was going nowhere in particular, and then he saw what seemed to be a very pretty nun walking down the road. He pulled over to pick her up and she gratefully accepted the lift, having walked over a mile already. As soon as she climbed into the van the man asked her a question that came into his mind.

"How do you nuns do that?" he asked.

"Do what?" she said.

"Manage to live with not having sex all those years?"

"I've been a nun for 25 years and I haven't done it yet, but now that you mention it, I suddenly realize I do want to."

The man was totally overcome with the same urge, so they climbed into the back of the van.

He agreed to have sex with her so that she could still be tested as a virgin. As soon as they climbed back into the front of the van, the man sighed and said, "I have a confession to make, I'm happily married with three kids."

The nun then said, "I have a confession to make, too! My name is really Harry and I'm on my way to a fancy-dress party."

Once upon a time there was a girl named Cinderella, who lived with her wicked step-mother and three step-sisters. When Prince Charming held a grand ball to find his true beloved, the wicked step-mother refused to let Cinderella go.

Alone and helpless, Cinderella could only cry silently.

Then suddenly her fairy godmother turned up. From various bits and pieces that Cinderella picked up around the house, the fairy godmother gave her everything she needed for the ball.

A collection of rags and various knick-knacks were turned into a beautiful ball gown and some of the world's best jewellery. Mice were turned into prancing white horses. A large pumpkin was turned into a coach.

The two old cats were turned into a groom and a footman.

"Oh, thank you, fairy godmother, but I just have one small problem." Cinderella confided that she was in the middle of having her period.

Looking around, they saw that there is nothing left in the house but there was a watermelon in the garden. The fairy godmother promptly turned this into a tampon.

"....and that is how Cinderella died at the stroke of midnight, Your Honour."

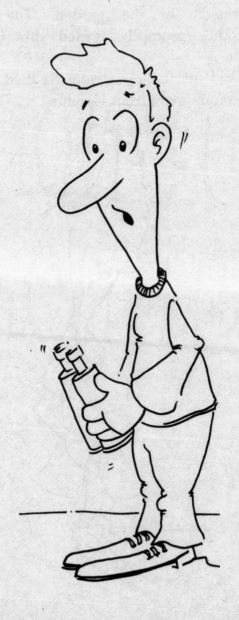

QUESTIONS, QUESTIONS!

Q. Why did the gay man put sunflower seeds up his ass?
A. Because gerbils have to eat too.

Q. What do blondes say during sex?
A. "Are you all on the same team?"

Q. Why are blondes so quiet when they have sex?
A. They don't talk to strangers.

Q. Why do blondes wear underwear?
A. To keep their ankles warm.

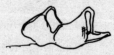

Q. How does a blonde turn on the lights after having sex?
A. She opens the car door.

Q. What does a blonde put behind her ears to attract men?
A. Her ankles.

Q. Why did the condom fly across the room?
A. Because it got pissed off.

Q. Why don't debutantes like gang-bangs?
A. Too many thank-you notes to write.

Q. What's the difference between a clitoris and a pub?
A. Men can always find a pub.

Q. Why doesn't Santa Claus have any children?
A. Because he only comes once a year.

Q. What's the worse thing about oral sex?
A. The view.

Q. Why do mutes masturbate with only one hand?
A. So they can moan with the other.

Q. What's the difference between condoms and coffins?
A. They both hold something stiff but one's coming and one's going!

Q. Why does Barbie never get pregnant?
A. Because Ken always comes in a box!

Q: What is the difference between ooh and aah?
A: About three inches.

Q. What's the Ultimate Rejection?
A. When you're masturbating, and your hand falls asleep.

Q. Why do women still like to have a man around?
A. Because vibrators can't mow the lawn.

WHAT'S UP DOC?

An 80-year-old man walked into a fertility clinic with his beloved 75-year-old wife. He went up to the doctor and told him of their plan to have another child.

The doctor told the man he would need a sperm sample to see if that was possible. He handed the old man a plastic jar and told him where to go.

The old boy took his wife by the hand and headed for a private room.

Two hours later the doctor was beginning to wonder if they would ever come out. The two finally emerged looking embarrassed.

"I tried with my left hand, I tried with my right hand, my wife tried with her teeth in, and she tried with her teeth out," cried the man. "But we still can't get the stupid lid off this thing!"

At a medical convention, a male and female doctor started eyeing each other. The male doctor asked the woman doctor to dinner and she accepted.

As they sat down in the restaurant, she excused herself to go and wash her hands. After dinner, one thing lead to another and they ended up in her hotel bedroom.

Just as things got really passionate, the woman doctor paused and said, "I've just got to go and wash my hands!"

Once she came back, they resumed their passionate embraces. After their moment of bliss, she got up and said "I've just got to go and wash my hands!"

When she came back the male doctor said, "I bet you're a surgeon." She nodded and asked how he'd guessed.

"Easy, you're always washing your hands."

She then said, "I'll bet you're an anaesthetist."

Male Doctor, "Hey, how did you know?"

Female Doctor, "I didn't feel a thing."

A promising young Californian medical student decided to specialize in sexual disorders and went to visit the hospital which had just accepted him as an intern.

One of the resident physicians took him on a tour of the hospital. They passed a cubicle with a young man in it who was masturbating furiously.

Turning to his superior, the intern asked about the man's problem.

The resident responded, "Oh, that man has an enormously over-active sex drive and he has to have 20 orgasms a day or he becomes seriously ill."

They moved on through the hospital and eventually come upon another man in a cubicle with his pants down around his ankles and a beautiful blonde nurse on her knees in front of him having enthusiastic oral sex with him.

The intern asked what this man's problem was. The resident replied,

"Same problem, better health plan."

"Doctor," the anxious young woman said, "I'm getting married this weekend and my fiancé thinks I'm a virgin. Is there anything you can do to help me?"

"Medically, no," he replied, "But here's a good suggestion: on your wedding night, when you're getting ready for bed, slide an elastic band around your upper thigh. When your husband enters you, snap the band and tell him it's your virginity snapping."

After the ceremony, the newly-weds retired to the honeymoon suite. The new bride undressed in the bathroom, slid the elastic band around her leg and climbed into bed.

They began to make love and, when her husband entered her, she snapped the elastic band.

"What the hell was that?" the startled fellow asked.

"Oh, that was just my virginity snapping, darling," she replied.

"Well snap it again," he groaned. "It's got my balls!"

A beautiful, voluptuous woman went to the gynaecologist.

The doctor took one look at her and all his professionalism went out the window.

Straight away, he told her to undress.

After she took all her clothes off, he began to stroke her thigh.

As he was doing this, he said to the woman, "Do you know what I'm doing?"

"Yes," she said, "You're checking for any abrasions or dermatological abnormalities."

"That is correct," said the doctor.

He then began to fondle her breasts. "Do you know what I'm doing now?" he asked.

"Yes," said the woman, "You're checking for any lumps or breast cancer."

"That's right," replied the doctor.

He then began to have sex with her.

He said, "Do you know what I'm doing now?"

"Yes," she replied, "You're getting herpes."

A man went to a plastic surgeon to have some surgery on his penis. The doctor, filled with curiosity, asked what on earth had happened to it.

"Well," the patient said, "I live in a caravan park, and this gorgeous, sexy woman lives in the caravan next to mine. I used to spy on her on her in her caravan and I saw that she had a very odd habit.

Every afternoon she used to take a hot dog from her refrigerator and put it in a hole on her caravan floor. Then she'd sit on it and have a wonderful time. She nearly drove me crazy!

So I got this bright idea. One day I crawled under her caravan and when she put the hot dog in the hole, I took it out and slipped my cock up through the hole instead.

She sat down on it and everything was just brilliant until there was a knock at the door."

"And then?" enquired the doctor.

"And then," the patient explained, "That was when she tried to kick it under the sofa."

BLESS ME, FATHER!

A young man went into the pharmacy to buy condoms. The assistant told him that the condoms came in packs of 3, 9 or 12 and asked which the young man wanted.

"Well", he said, "I've been seeing this girl for quite a while and she's really sexy. I want the condoms because I think tonight's going to be THE night. We're having dinner with her parents, and then we're going out.

Once she's had sex with me, she'll want me all the time, so I think you'd better give me the 12-pack."

The young man bought the condoms and went home.

Later that evening, he sat down to dinner with his girlfriend and her parents. Much to his girlfriend's surprise, he asked if he might give the blessing, and her parents agreed.

He began to say grace, but carried on praying for several minutes. The girl leaned over to him and said, "You never told me that you were such a religious person."

He leaned over to her and whispered,

"You never told me that your father is a pharmacist!"

There were three men who died and went to heaven. The first man went up to see God who said, "You have committed adultery so I'm giving you a push-bike."

The second man went up and God said,

"You have almost committed adultery so I'm giving you a motorcycle."

The third man went up and God said to him,

"You have only thought about adultery, so you'll get a Porsche!"

The first man came up to the man in the Porsche and started laughing, so the man in the Porsche asked,

"Why are you laughing at me? You only got a push-bike!"

The man on the push-bike replied,

"I just saw your wife on a skateboard!"

Two nuns were riding a bike down a road and the first nun said, "I've never come this way before!"

The second nun replied, "Oh, it must be the cobblestones!"

A local vicar was paying a visit to one of his church members on a Friday night, and heard a loud party in progress as he approached the house.

He knocked on the door and the owner answered.

Behind him, he saw a circle of naked men, with blindfolded women moving from man to man. They were fondling each man's cock and guessing who it belonged to.

The vicar, seeing this, said, "I'm sorry, I don't think I'd fit in here at the moment"

"Nonsense," the man replied, "Your name's been called three times already!"

It was time for Father John's Saturday night bath and young Sister Magdalene had prepared the bath water and towels just the way the old nun had instructed.

Sister Magdalene was also told never to look at Father John's naked body if she could help it, to do whatever he told her and to pray constantly.

The next morning the old nun asked Sister Magdalene how the Saturday night bath had gone.

"Oh, sister," said the young nun dreamily. "I've been saved."

"Saved? And how did that fine thing come about?" asked the old nun.

"Well, when Father John was soaking in the bath, he asked me to wash him and, while I was washing him, he guided my hand down between his legs, where he said the Lord keeps the Key to Heaven."

"Did he now?" said the old nun evenly.

Sister Magdalene continued, "And Father John said that if the Key to Heaven fitted my lock, the portals of Heaven would be opened to me and I would be assured of salvation and eternal peace.

And then Father John guided his Key to Heaven into my lock."

"Is that a fact?" said the old nun even more evenly.

"At first it hurt terribly, but Father John said the pathway to salvation was often painful and that the glory of God would soon swell my heart with ecstasy. And so it did! It felt so good, being saved."

"That wicked old Devil," said the old nun. "He told me it was Gabriel's Horn, and I've been blowing it for 40 years!"

Priest: "Do you shrink from making love?"
Girl: "If I did, I'd be a midget!"

To me a woman's body is a temple – and I try to attend services as often as possible.

MECHANICAL AIDS

A businessman was going on a long business trip. He knew his wife was very flirtatious, so he thought he'd try to get her something to keep her occupied while he was gone, because he didn't like the idea of her having sex with someone else.

He went to a shop that sold sex toys and started looking around. He thought about the life-sized sex doll, but he thought it was too similar to a real man.

He started browsing through the dildos next, looking for something special to please his wife, and started talking to the old man behind the counter. He explained his situation.

The old man said, "Well, I don't really know of anything that will do the trick. We have vibrating dildos, special attachments, and so on, but I don't know of anything that will keep her occupied for weeks, except ," and he stopped.

"Except what?" the man asked.

"Nothing, nothing."

"Come on, tell me! I need something desperately!"

"Well, sir, I don't usually tell people about this, but there is the 'voodoo dick'."

"So, what is this voodoo dick?" the man

asked. The old man reached under the counter, and pulled out a wooden box, carved with strange symbols.

He opened it, and there lay a very ordinary-looking dildo.

The businessman laughed, and said, "Really! It looks like every other dildo in this shop!"

The old man replied, "But you haven't seen what it'll do yet." He pointed to the door and said, "Voodoo dick, the door!"

The voodoo dick rose out of its box, darted over to the door, and started having sex with the keyhole. The whole door shook with the vibrations, and a crack developed down the middle. Before the door looked like it was going to split in half, the old man said,

"Voodoo dick, box!" The voodoo dick stopped, floated back to the box and lay there, quiescent once more.

"I'll take it!" said the businessman. The old man demurred, saying it really wasn't for sale, but he finally surrendered it for £500 in cash.

The man took the dildo home to his wife, told her it was a very special dildo and that to use it, all she had to do was say "Voodoo dick, my pussy!"

He left for his business trip satisfied that everything would be fine while he was gone. After he'd been gone a few days, the wife was feeling unbearably sexy. She thought of several people who would willingly satisfy her, but then she remembered the voodoo dick. She got it out, and said, "Voodoo dick, my pussy!"

The voodoo dick immediately started having sex with her. It was amazing, like nothing she'd ever experienced before. After three orgasms, she decided she'd had enough, and tried to pull it out, but it was stuck inside her, still carrying on. She tried and tried to get it out, but nothing worked. Her husband had forgotten to tell her how to shut it off.

So she decided to go to the hospital to see if they could help. She put her clothes on, got in the car and started to drive to the hospital, quivering with every thrust of the dildo.

On the way, a violent orgasm nearly made her swerve off the road, and she was pulled over by a policeman. He asked for her licence, and then asked how much she'd had to drink.

Gasping and twitching, she explained that she hadn't been drinking, but that a voodoo dick was stuck inside her, and wouldn't stop having sex with her.

The officer looked at her sceptically, and then said:

"Yeah, right......... Voodoo dick, my ass!"

When he passed her bedroom, a father saw his daughter having sex with the aid of a vibrator.

"What on earth are you doing?" he said.

"Well, dad! I'm 30 years old, fat, ugly and I've never even had a boyfriend. There's no way I'll ever get married, so this electronic device is my substitute husband," replied the daughter.

Several days later, the daughter came home from work and saw her dad sitting in a chair, watching television.

He had a beer in one hand and her vibrator in the other.

"What's going on?" she asks.

"I'm just having a beer with my son-in-law," he said.

Some time ago, there was a man who went to Vietnam and got his arm blown off in a major battle. He went back to the United States a year later and talked to an old friend about his troubles. His friend told him about a new invention. The invention was a mechanical arm that did everything you told it to do.

The man was a little nervous about the idea but he decided to have a go with it. So a month later he got the mechanical arm attached and returned home for the first time.

He got to the front door and said, "Open the door!" The arm opened the door for him.

Then he said, "Close the door." The arm closed the door.

Later on that evening he was watching T.V. and wanted a beer, so he walked to the fridge and said, "Open the refrigerator and take me out a beer." The arm opened the door and got him a beer.

The man was delighted with the arm. About an hour later he was desperate for a piss. He went to the bathroom and said, "Unzip my flies and take my cock out."

The arm did as instructed, the man had a piss and, when he'd finished, he said, "Shake it a bit." The arm obeyed.

Well, he thought that felt quite good, so he said,

"Shake it again, harder." Well, he thought, that felt really good, so he said, "Jerk me off." The arm then proceeded to pull his cock off. The man screamed "Oh, f**k me." Then the arm put it up his rear. The man roared, "Oh, I can't believe what I'm seeing!"

So the arm shoved his cock in his eye.

WEDDED BLISS

A wife was cleaning out the wardrobe and right at the top of the top shelf she notices a large box. She carefully takes the box down and notices a sign on it which reads: DO NOT OPEN!

Naturally she was curious, so she opened the box and inside she found £10,000 in cash and three golf balls.

Later that evening her husband came home, and she immediately confronted him about the contents of the box.

The husband was very upset, but his wife asked, "Why are there three golf balls in the box?"

"Every time we had bad sex I put a golf ball in the box," the husband replied.

"Hmm, three golf balls, 20 years of marriage, that's not bad," she thought.

"So what's the £10,000 for?," she asked.

"Every time I got a dozen golf balls, I sold them."

First woman: "I never made love to my husband before we got married. How about you?"

Second woman: "I don't know. What's his name?"

On her wedding night, the young bride took her mother aside and said, "Ma, tell me how to make my new husband happy."

Her mother replied, "Well, when two people love each other, they make love."

"Oh, I know all about that, Ma," the bride responded. "I want to know how to make lasagne."

A man came home from work one day and gave his wife a dozen yellow roses. The next day, his wife was hanging out the washing in the back garden, and chatting to her neighbour over the fence.

"Yesterday", she said, "the old man gave me a dozen yellow roses, and now I suppose he expects me to lie on my back with my legs in the air for a week!"

"Why?" replied the neighbour, "don't you have a vase?"

A newly wed couple went to bed early on Christmas night.

The wife woke up in the middle of the night,

shook her husband awake and said: "Darling, Darling, wake up! I had the most amazing dream!"

Husband: "What? What was it?"

Wife: "In my dream I saw a Christmas tree that was decorated with lots of different kinds of cocks. There were big ones, small ones, black ones, white ones, and at the top of the tree was the most perfect one: it was really long and thick!"

Husband: "But of course, it was my cock, wasn't it?"

Wife: "No, it was John Parker's!"

The husband, annoyed that his wife had woken up him to tell him that she'd had a dream about John Parker's cock, rolled over and went back to sleep.

Later he woke up, shook his wife and said:

"Dearest, I had the most amazing dream!"

Wife: "What was it?"

Husband: "In my dream I saw a Christmas tree that was decorated with lots of different kinds of pussys. There were tight ones, loose ones, black ones, white ones, and at the very top of the tree was the perfect pussy: it was so tight and sweetly shaped!"

Wife: "Well, it must have been mine!"

Husband: "No, dearest! yours was holding the tree up!"

A man and his wife had been stranded on a desert island for many years. One day another man was washed up on shore. He and the wife were very attracted to each other right away, but realized that certain protocols must be observed.

The husband, however, was very glad to see the second man there. "Now we will be able to have three people doing eight hour shifts in the watchtower, rather than two people doing 12-hour shifts." The new man was only too happy to help out and volunteered to do the next shift. He climbed up the tower and began standing watch.

Soon the husband and wife started placing stones in a circle to make a fire to cook supper. The second man yelled down, "Hey, no sex down there!" They yelled back, "We're not having sex!"

A few minutes later they started to put driftwood into the stone circle. Again the second man yelled down, "Hey, no f**king!"

Again they yelled back, "We're not f**king!"

Later they were putting palm leaves on the roof of their shack to patch leaks. Once again the second man yelled down, "Hey, I said no sex!" They shouted back, "We're not having sex!"

Finally his shift was over so the second man climbed down from the tower and the husband climbed up to take his turn on watch. He wasn't even halfway up before the wife and second man are having passionate sex.

The husband looked down from the tower and said to himself, "My God! From up here it really DOES look as though they're f**king."

The man and woman had been married for quite a time. One day the husband, thinking he was being funny, grabbed his wife's boobs as she was getting into the shower and said to her,

"You know, if these were really firm, you wouldn't need a bra!" The wife became angry; it was such a horrible thing to say. The next day, as she was getting out of the shower, he grabbed her bottom and said,

"You know, if this was really firm, you wouldn't need a girdle!" Now the wife was really angry and started plotting her revenge.

The next day, as her husband was getting out of the shower, she grabbed his cock and said, "You know, if this was really firm I wouldn't need your brother!"

Jane was a first -time contestant on a quiz show, where you have to answer questions to win the cash prize.

Lady luck had smiled on her, so Jane had gained a substantial lead over her opponents. She even managed to win the game but, unfortunately, time ran out before the show's host could ask her the final £100,000 question.

Needless to say, Jane agreed to return the following day. She was nervous and fidgety as her husband drove them home.

"I've just got to win tomorrow," she said, "I wish I knew what the answers are. I'm not going to be able to sleep at all tonight. I will probably look terrible tomorrow."

"Relax, dear," her husband, Mike, reassured her,

"It will all be OK."

Ten minutes after they arrived home, Mike

grabbed the car keys and started heading for the door.

"Where are you going?" Jane asked.

"I have a little errand to run. I should be back soon," he replied.

Jane waited impatiently for Mike's return. After an agonizing three-hour absence, Mike returned, sporting a very wide and wicked grin. "Honey, I managed to get tomorrow's question and answer!" he exclaimed.

"What is it?" she cried excitedly.

"OK. The question is 'What are the three main parts of the male anatomy?' And the answer is 'The head, the heart, and the penis."

Shortly after that, the couple went to sleep, and Jane, now feeling confident and at ease, plummeted into a deep and restful slumber.

At 3:30 in the morning, however, Jane was shaken awake by Mike, who was asking her the big quiz show question. "The head, the heart, and the penis," Jane replied groggily before returning to sleep. And Mike asked her again in the morning, this time as Jane was brushing her teeth. Once again, Jane answered correctly.

Jane was once again was sitting on the set of the quiz show. Even though she knew both the question and answer, she could feel the butterflies in her stomach and terror running through her veins. The cameras started rolling and the host, after reminding the audience of the previous day's events, faced Jane and asked the big question.

"Jane, for £100,000, what are the main parts of the male anatomy? You have 10 seconds."

"Hmm, uhm, the head?" she said nervously.

"Very good. Six seconds."

"Eh, uh, the heart?"

Very good! Four seconds."

"I, uhh, oooooooohh, darn! My husband drilled it into me last night and I had it on the tip of my tongue this morning..."

"That's close enough," said the game show host,"

CONGRATULATIONS! You have won £100,000."

A married man gets home early from work and hears strange noises coming from the bedroom. He rushes upstairs to find his wife naked on the bed, sweating and panting.

"What's up?" he asks.

"I'm having a heart attack," cries the woman.

He rushes downstairs to grab the phone, but just as he's dialling, his 4-year-old son comes up and says,

"Daddy! Daddy! Uncle Ted's hiding in your closet and he's got no clothes on!" The man slams the phone down and storms upstairs into the bedroom, past his screaming wife, and rips open the wardrobe door. Sure enough, there is his brother, totally naked, cowering on the closet floor.

"You bastard!" says the husband. "My wife's having a heart attack, and all you can do is run around the house naked scaring the kids?"

A woman was in bed, having sex with her husband's best friend when all of a sudden the telephone rings and she answers.

After hanging up she says, "That was Harry, but don't worry, he won't be home for a while. He's playing cards with you."

An escaped convict broke into a house and tied up a young couple who had been sleeping in the bedroom. As soon as he had a chance, the husband turned to his voluptuous young wife, bound up on the bed in a skimpy nightgown, and whispered,

"Honey, this guy hasn't seen a woman in years. Just cooperate with anything he wants. If he wants to have sex with you, you just go along with it and pretend you like it. Our lives depend on it."

"Dearest," his wife hissed, spitting out her gag, "I'm so relieved you feel that way, because he just told me he thinks you have a really cute looking ass."

A husband and wife were in the bathroom getting ready to go to work when the husband looked at his wife and said, "I've just got to have you right now!"

He backed her up against the bathroom door, pulled down her knickers and had sex with her.

When they had finished, he started putting his clothes back on and saw his wife still writhing around against the door.

He asked, "What's wrong, honey? Didn't you come? Do you want more?"

His wife said, "No, no, it's not that. I'm just trying to get the door knob out of my behind"

Two men were discussing the new secretary at their office.

John said to George, "Man, I went out with her last Tuesday and we had wonderful sex. She's a lot better in bed than my wife!" Two days later, George said to John, "Well, I went out with her too and we had sex as well, but she certainly isn't that much better than your wife."

One night, a flying saucer lands in Dallas, Texas, in the back garden of a fun-loving married couple called Bob and Pat. A male and female alien emerge from the flying saucer and introduce themselves as being from Mars. They tell Bob and Pat that they came to Earth for an experiment. Tim asked, "What do you want from us?"

The aliens replied that they wanted to see what it was like to have sex with an earthling, and if the two of them would like to participate in their experiment. Bob and Pat thought it over and agree to give it a go. Bob took the female into one bedroom, while Pat took the male into another bedroom. As soon as the male alien was undressed, Pat looked at him and started laughing. The alien asked, "What's so funny?"

Pat replied, "I'm sorry, I shouldn't have laughed, but I just don't think you're large enough to satisfy any woman here on Earth!"

The alien replied, "No problem, watch this." He pulled on his ears and his cock quickly grew to ten inches.

Pat smiled and said, "Now, that's more like it!"

A few hours later, after the aliens had gone back to Mars, Bob asked Pat, "Did you enjoy sex with the alien OK, dear?"

"It was fantastic," replied a very happy Pat. Pat then returned the question, "How about you dear – did you enjoy sex with your alien?"

"It was fine," Bob replied, I just wish she'd stop pulling on my ears, though!"

There were these two Americans who played golf together every Saturday. Well, one Saturday they were getting ready to tee off when a guy on his own asked if he could join them.

The friends looked at each other and then looked at the man and said it was OK. So they teed off.

About two holes into the game, the friends got curious to know what the man did for a living. So they asked him. The stranger told them that he was a hit-man. The friends kind of laughed. The man said, "No really, I am a hit-man. My gun is in my golf bag. I carry it everywhere I go. You can take a look if you like."

So one of the men decided he would. He opened up the bag and, sure enough, there was this rifle with a huge telescopic sight on it. He got all excited about it. He said, "WOW! I bet I can see my house through this! May I look?"

The stranger handed him the rifle. The man looked through the sight and said, "YEAH! You can! I can even see through my windows into my bedroom. There's my wife, naked. Isn't she beautiful? WAIT THOUGH! There's my next door neighbour! He's naked too!" This so upset the man that he asked the hit-man how much it would be to do a hit.

The hit man replied, "It's $1000 every time I

pull the trigger."

The man said, "$1000, WOW! Well, OK. I want two hits. I want you to shoot my wife right in the mouth. She is always nagging at me and I can't stand it. Second, I want you to shoot my neighbour right in the cock, just for screwing around with my wife."

The hit-man agreed so he sets the gun up and looks through the scope. He was looking steadily for about 5 minutes. The man started to get impatient and asked the hit-man what he was waiting for. The hit-man replied,

"Just hold on a second... I'm about to save you a thousand bucks."